TIME FOR KIDS

Physical Feats & Failures

Dona Herweck Rice

Consultants

Timothy Rasinski, Ph.D.
Kent State University

Lori Oczkus
Literacy Consultant

Based on writing from *TIME For Kids. TIME For Kids* and the *TIME For Kids* logo are registered trademarks of TIME Inc. Used under license.

Publishing Credits

Dona Herweck Rice, *Editor-in-Chief*
Lee Aucoin, *Creative Director*
Jamey Acosta, *Senior Editor*
Lexa Hoang, *Designer*
Stephanie Reid, *Photo Editor*
Rachelle Cracchiolo, *M.S.Ed., Publisher*

Image Credits: cover, pp.1, 11 REUTERS/ Newscom; p.8 Bettmann/Corbis/AP Images; p.40 (middle) Associated Press; pp.6–7 Jerry Cooke/Corbis; p.37 (bottom) Bmtlines/ Dreamstime; pp.7 (bottom), 16–19, 24–25, 32 Getty Image; p.5 (top) ABC via Getty Images; p.33 (bottom) LOC [LC-USZC4-7246]; p.35 (top) Action Plus/Newscom; p.36 (top) Action Press/Newscom; p.15 (top) AFP/Getty Images/ Newscom; p.21–22 AFP/Newscom; p.30–31 cs9/ ZUMA Press/Newscom; p.12–13, 33–34 Empics/ Newscom; p.28–29 Josh Chapel/Southcreek Global/Newscom; pp.15 (bottom), 33–34 KRT/ Newscom; p.30 Louis Lopez/Cal Sport Media/ Newscom; p.26–27 LVNB/Newscom; p.34 MCT/ Newscom; p.14, 32–33, 40 (top) Newscom; p.29 (left) Scott A. Tugel/Newscom; pp.10 (top & bottom), 40–41 (bottom) ZUMA Press/ Newscom; pp.12, 41 (top) UPI/Newscom; pp.16, 17 (bottom), 36 (bottom) WENN/Newscom; p.37 (top) Xinhua/Photoshot/Newscom; All other images from Shutterstock.

Teacher Created Materials
5301 Oceanus Drive
Huntington Beach, CA 92649-1030
http://www.tcmpub.com

ISBN 978-1-4333-4870-9

Table of Contents

One Foot in Front of the Other

When a baby toddles on its little legs and takes its first step, there is no doubt it has achieved a **feat** worth celebrating. After all, it took a lot of falling down and try-try-again spirit to get to that single step! Through time, babies everywhere have done what they have to do to get the job done. Their efforts seem to be a part of the human spirit. And their achievements don't stop with a single step!

People around the world go from walking to running, jumping, flipping, spinning, and even flying in ways that seem superhuman. How do they do it? The secret to their success is the same as the drive inside that baby working up to its first step. Try and try. Believe you can do it. Go for it. Then, success!

Or not. The truth is, for every awesome physical feat, there are many failures. But the failures can make the feats seem even sweeter. The world has known many mind-blowing feats. And it has known many heartbreaking, bone-crushing failures. But no matter what happens, just as with babies, people get up, get out, and get the job done.

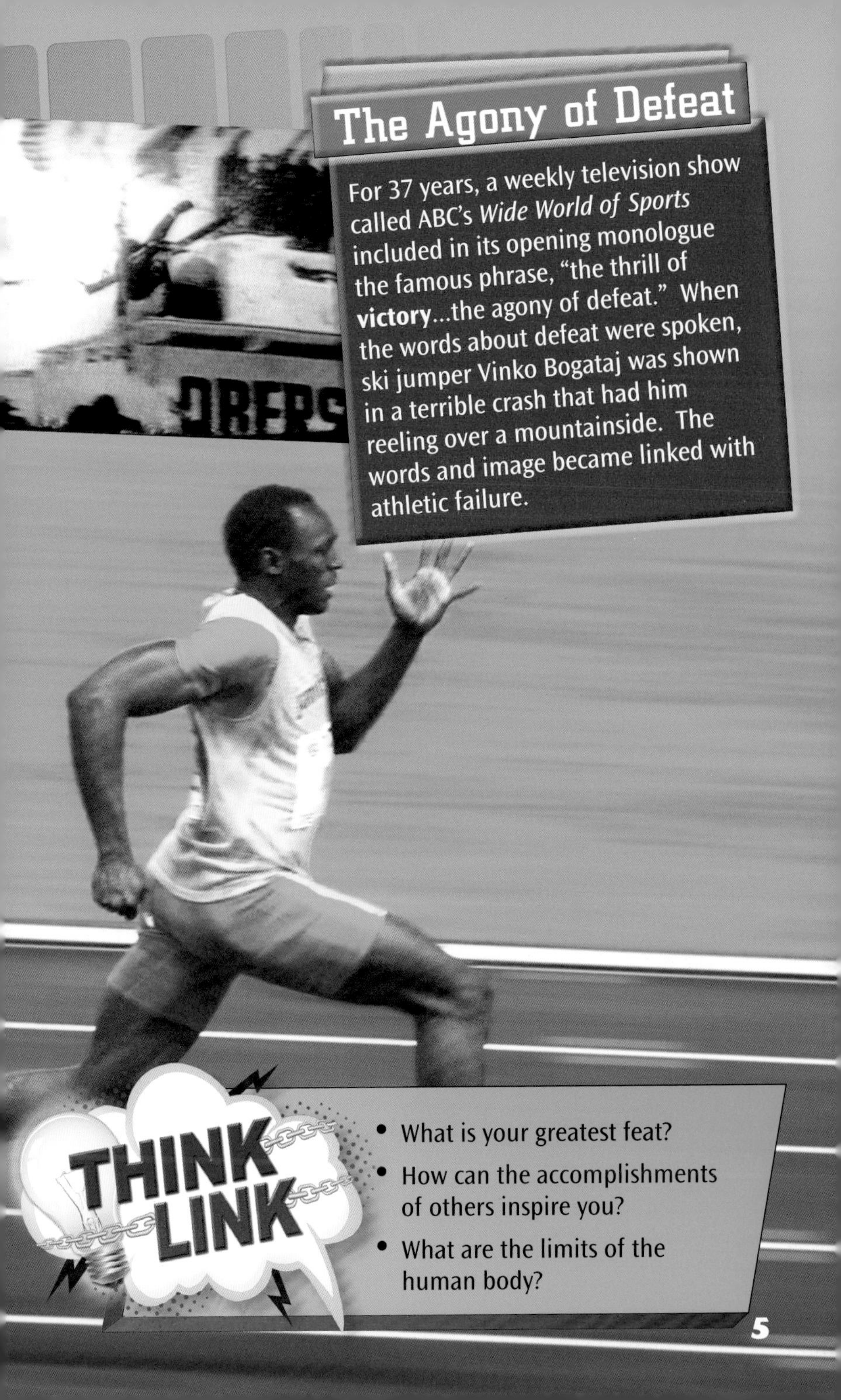

The Agony of Defeat

For 37 years, a weekly television show called ABC's *Wide World of Sports* included in its opening monologue the famous phrase, "the thrill of **victory**...the agony of defeat." When the words about defeat were spoken, ski jumper Vinko Bogataj was shown in a terrible crash that had him reeling over a mountainside. The words and image became linked with athletic failure.

THINK LINK

- What is your greatest feat?
- How can the accomplishments of others inspire you?
- What are the limits of the human body?

The Fastest Woman in the World

In 1960, Wilma Rudolph was called the Fastest Woman in the World. She set world records and won three gold medals for track and field. People were awed by her speed and skill. Little did they know that when Rudolph was very young, she could not even walk on her own.

Rudolph was born too early and was a sickly child. She had **polio** when she was four years old. The disease left her left leg and foot twisted. Her mother spent hours with Rudolph, helping to straighten her leg and improve its use. Rudolph needed leg massages several times a day. She wore a brace on her leg for three years. Finally, when she was 12, Rudolph could walk like other children.

Rudolph and her mother took a 50-mile bus trip every week for special treatments.

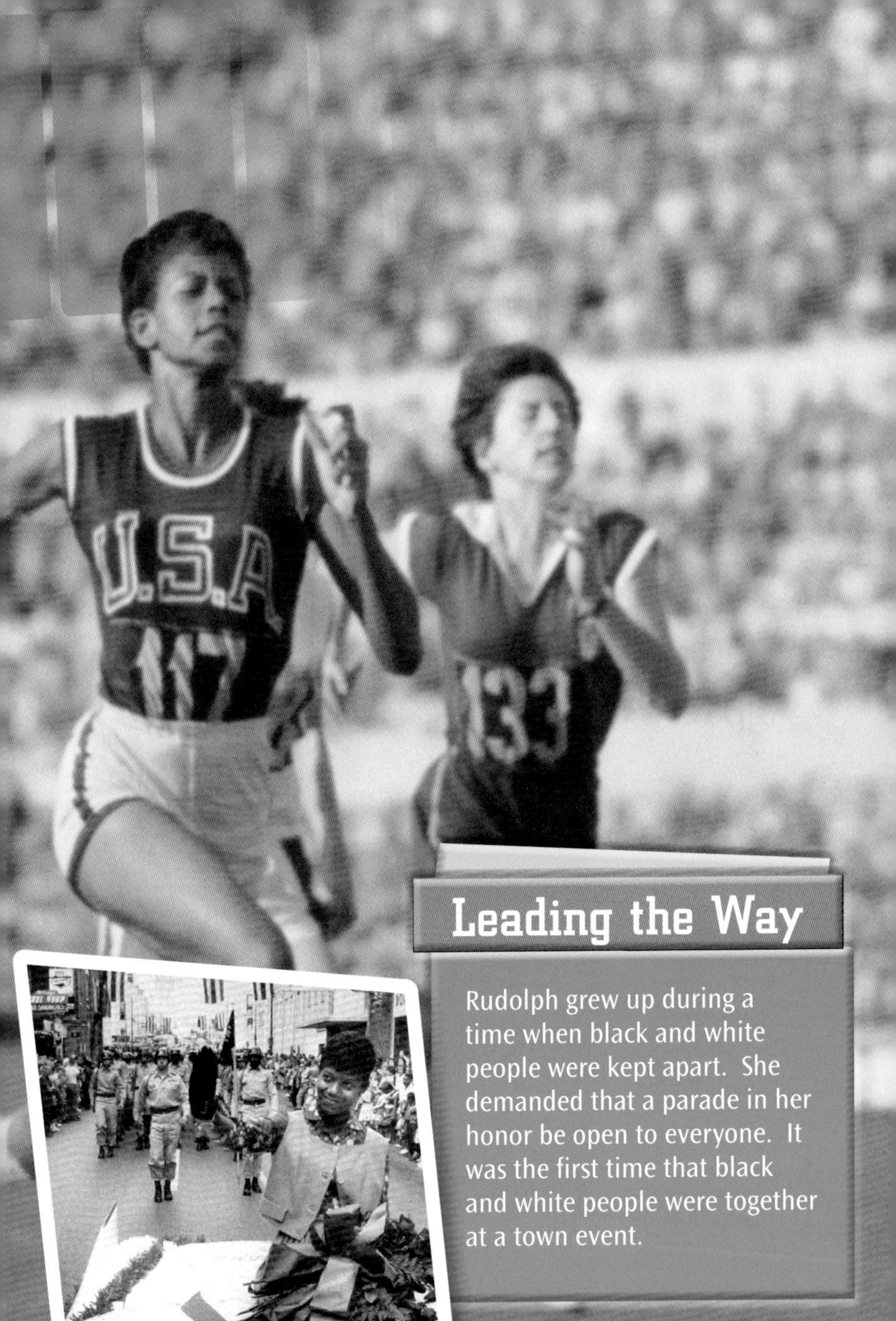

Leading the Way

Rudolph grew up during a time when black and white people were kept apart. She demanded that a parade in her honor be open to everyone. It was the first time that black and white people were together at a town event.

One of Rudolph's sisters was a basketball star. Rudolph wanted to do that, too. So, with practice and **determination**, she became a success on the court. A **scout** for track and field spotted her there.

Rudolph made the U.S. Olympic track and field team in 1956 at age 16. In 1960, she won her gold medals. She also won the praise of the world!

Racetrack Math

Runners apply force to the ground. The success of each step can be measured by how force is applied. Steps that are 100 percent **efficient** waste no energy.

If the heel touches the ground, the steps are slower. Missteps can make runners only 70 percent efficient.

If an athlete falls to the ground, the step is completely inefficient.

0% potential force used

Rudolph had 22 brothers and sisters. That's an amazing feat for her parents!

If an athlete doesn't push off from the ground hard enough, only 80 percent of potential energy is being used.

The perfect step, or stride, results in 100 percent of potential force being used.

Man or Fish?

As long as people have been walking, they have been swimming, too. Like many other species, people have fun in the water. But some people take to the water as though they are fish. People around the world know Michael Phelps. And many of them joke that Phelps must be related to some type of fish species. They say he moves as if he has fins.

Phelps's awards for swimming are unmatched. He has the most wins of any athlete in World Championship history. He also has the most medal wins at a single Olympics. He took home eight gold medals during the 2004 games! And he is the youngest man to set a world record. He broke the 200-meter fly mark at the 2001 Spring Nationals at age 15. The list of awards and medals goes on and on. As of today, there seems to be no end in sight!

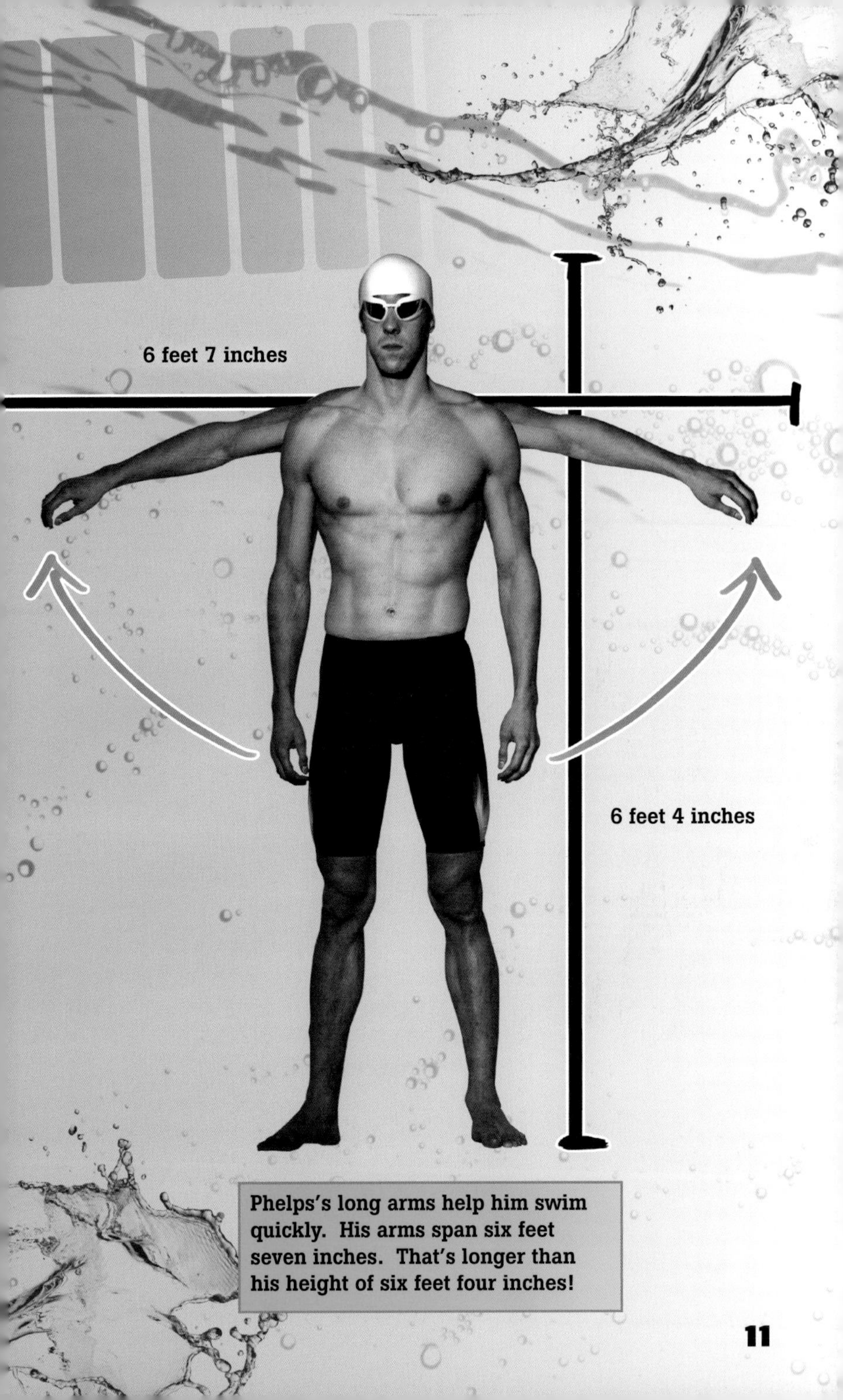

Phelps's long arms help him swim quickly. His arms span six feet seven inches. That's longer than his height of six feet four inches!

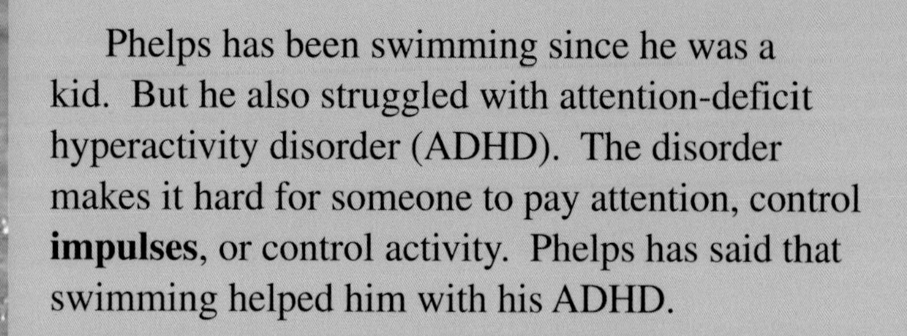

Phelps has been swimming since he was a kid. But he also struggled with attention-deficit hyperactivity disorder (ADHD). The disorder makes it hard for someone to pay attention, control **impulses**, or control activity. Phelps has said that swimming helped him with his ADHD.

Kerri Strug

Everyone who saw her perform was amazed! Standing on a hurt ankle, Olympic gymnast Kerri Strug began her sprint to the vault, where she sprang off both ankles to earn a score of 9.712. That was enough to earn the U.S. women's team the gold medal. As soon as Strug landed on both feet, she quickly hopped up on one foot and then fell to her knees. She was in terrible pain, but like the best athletes, she did what she needed to do to become a champion.

DON'T Try This at Home

In 2007, performer David Blaine attempted to break the world record for holding his breath. He failed and was forced to give up. But a year later, he worked with doctors to hold his breath for over 17 minutes. Before attempting the stunt, he breathed pure oxygen. But it was still very dangerous.

At age 15, Phelps became the youngest male in history to set a swimming world record.

Olympic Feats and Failures

It starts with talent and ends with determination—and maybe a bit of luck. These amazing athletes have achieved what most of us would find impossible. Or they have failed in heartbreaking ways, despite their best efforts.

Greg Louganis

In a move that sent chills through viewers everywhere, Olympic high-diver Greg Louganis (loo-GEY-ness) cracked his head on the diving board during the **preliminaries**. If hit the wrong way, the knock could have killed Louganis. But after getting stitches, he came back for his next dive and scored the highest marks that day. On the next day, during the finals, Louganis took home the gold medal.

Are these the best—or saddest—stories? No, every four years the Olympics is filled with new triumphs and tragedies. These are just some of the stories.

Karnam Malleswari

Karnam Malleswari (kar-nahm maof India entered Olympic history when she became the first Indian woman to win a medal in weight lifting. She was also India's first woman to win a medal—ever! Malleswari won her bronze medal in 2000.

Derek Redmond

Derek Redmond of Britain had to withdraw from the 1992 Summer Olympics when he tore his hamstring during a **semifinal** race. Although Redmond didn't win a medal, he did inspire everyone as he struggled to finish the race. When he couldn't, his father came from the stands to help his son all the way to the finish line.

Han Xiaopeng

China is not known for its skiing, but in the 2006 Winter Olympics, Han Xiaopeng (shou-PING) of China won a gold medal. No one in China had ever gone to the finals in a Winter Olympic event. But not only did he go to the finals, he took home the gold! He was also the youngest gold medalist in Olympic snow skiing history and set a world record at the same time.

Legless, Fearless

Some athletes have come back to peak fitness after injury. Others have risen to the top of their field with bodies that seemed limited from the start. One such athlete and inspiration is Aimee Mullins.

Because she was born without important bones in her lower legs, Mullins's legs were removed below the knee as a baby. But Mullins was strong and confident, and she had a great attitude. Using **prosthetic** (pros-THET-ik) legs, she became a top track-and-field athlete.

Mullins now works as a fashion model. She walks the runway for well-known designers. She even models for a famous makeup company.

Anthony Robles

A college-level wrestling champ, Anthony Robles was born with only one leg. Even as a young child, he didn't want to wear a prosthetic leg. He won his state wrestling title in both his junior and senior years of high school. In college, he became a national champion for 2010–2011 and finished his senior year of college undefeated. He is also a three-time All-American wrestling champion.

Mullins enjoys changing her height from five feet eight inches to over six feet by wearing different prosthetic legs.

Mullins walking the runway

Many people admire Mullins and her story. They want to know more about how she is able to accomplish so much. Mullins is happy to tell them. She is now a **motivational** speaker. She explains that her legs give her "super-powers." She doesn't see her legs as a problem. She sees them as a great gift. Mullins is not only a fashion model but also a model for living well!

When Words Fail Us

Sometimes, the only failure that happens is the way we describe something. When Mullins looked up *disabled* in the thesaurus, she was saddened to find these synonyms: *diseases*, *ill*, *unfit*, *sick*, *lame*, *unwell*, *unhealthy*. Those words didn't describe her. Mullins knew her amputation was only a failure to those who defined her by those terms.

To prevent dragging, the knee pulls the prosthetic leg up as the foot moves forward.

Step by Step

In 1999, Mullins was named one of the 50 most beautiful people in the world by *People* magazine.

On the Wire

From the first beams placed in 1966 until their terrible collapse on September 11, 2001, the twin towers of the World Trade Center watched over New York City like two giant guards. They were an amazing feat of engineering. But on August 7, 1974, people watching on the ground and from windows in nearby skyscrapers were stunned to see a cable stretched between the buildings. And standing in the middle of the cable, holding a heavy balancing bar—but with nothing else between him and a 1,368 foot drop—stood Philippe Petit (fil-EE-pay PEH-tee). He was a famous French performer and a master of the high wire. And he was walking on a cable between the two buildings.

On the Ground

Petit loved magic and juggling from an early age and started wire walking at age 16. Within a year, he mastered all the tricks. That was when he began inventing his own tricks. He made his living as a street artist and performed all over Europe.

How did Petit stretch the cable quickly and secretly between the two towers? He used a bow and arrows!
131 feet across
1,368 feet down

As people held their breath, Petit placed one foot in front of the other. Viewers gasped. They cheered. They covered their eyes and peeked between their fingers. And step by step, Petit did it. He reached the other side. And he reached it again. And again. Petit crossed eight times. He also lay down on the cable, danced, and leaped with both feet in the air!

Of course, the police were waiting for him. It wasn't legal to walk a tightwire between the towers. But even his arrest couldn't change the fact that Petit had done something almost no one on the planet could do—or would even dream of doing.

Amazing? Yes. But whether it was an amazing feat of courage or stupidity, only you can decide.

The Flying Wallendas

Considered by many to be the greatest circus performers of all time, the Flying Wallendas were a high-wire and **daredevil** act in the early 20th century. People came from all around to see their amazing stunts. But just one mistake ends the career of a high-wire artist. After more than 50 years performing, the group's founder, Karl Wallenda, died from a fall off the high wire at the age of 73.

Petit “walked” between the towers for 45 minutes before oncoming rain finally made him give up.

★ Pure Evel ★★

What does it take to turn your life around? With a tough childhood that began in 1938, Robert Craig Knievel (kih-NEE-vuhl) made some bad choices and served time in jail. A guard there gave him a nickname that stuck—Evel Knievel.

Knievel always loved thrills. He especially liked to watch daredevils. He began to perform fancy jumps on a bicycle. Later, he taught himself to jump on motorcycles.

As an adult, Knievel tried many jobs. He even served in the army. But the thrill of the jump always brought him back. In 1966, he started his own daredevil show.

Knievel was known for wearing American-themed caped outfits during his jumps.

Knievel was inducted into the Motorcycle Hall of Fame in 1999.

The *Guinness Book of World Records* named Knievel as the survivor of "the most broken bones in a lifetime."

Knievel gained fame on New Year's Eve 1967. That is when he jumped over the fountain outside Caesar's Palace in Las Vegas, Nevada. The stunt was shown on TV, and Knievel became famous. But he spent the next 29 days in a **coma**! It was an amazing feat and failure all at once.

Did that stop Knievel? No way! He jumped and jumped again in even more daring stunts. He wanted to jump the Grand Canyon, but no one would let him. Finally, he tried to jump the Snake River in Idaho instead. It failed when his safety chute opened right after takeoff.

Knievel's longest jump was over 14 buses. Between 1965 and 1981, he tried over 75 ramp-to-ramp jumps. And he broke 433 bones while doing it!

Ramp It Up!

The slope of a ramp is expressed as a percent. For example, a 25 percent sloped ramp goes up 25 feet every 100 feet. What is the slope of the ramp below?

100 feet

Knievel action figures were among the most popular toys for boys during his heyday in the 1970s.

Knievel's End

Although Knievel lived a dangerous life and was hospitalized many times, his profession didn't kill him. He died of lung disease at the age of 69.

Nitro Man

"Oh! Oh...my...word! Are you kidding me?" The announcer could barely speak the words. Travis Pastrana, age 22, had just made the first-ever double backflip in freestyle motocross at the 2006 X Games.

Just seconds earlier, Pastrana sat atop his bike at the top of the starting ramp. The crowd's cheers roared for this huge fan favorite. Countless camera flashes lit up the night sky. Pastrana revved his engine. Then, off he shot down the ramp, across the dirt, and up a small ramp. Up, up, up he sailed, flying his motorbike backward once...and then again! Down he landed, then up a ramp, where Pastrana jumped off and ran through the arena. He pumped his fists in victory to the crowd's screams. No one had ever done that before! They couldn't imagine doing it. But a young and fearless Pastrana made it happen. The crowd went wild!

Nitro Circus

Pastrana is the ringleader of the Nitro Circus, a group of professional action sport athletes. He is usually the first to try any dirt bike or BMX stunt.

The X Games were first called the Extreme Games because they included extreme sports like skateboarding and sport climbing.

People can't wait to see what Pastrana will do next. He has won two motocross racing titles. He is the four-in-a-row winner of the Rally America Driver's Championship. Add to that his 16 X-Games medals, and Pastrana is today's motorsport star!

X Games

Pastrana won the first-ever Moto X freestyle event at the X Games. In 2001, he was named Motocross Rider of the Year by ESPN. By 2005, he had won five gold medals in the X Games and five more at the Gravity Games.

Too Extreme!

In 2011, Pastrana broke his foot doing one of his signature moves. The accident forced him to bow out of the X Games. He felt like he had let everyone down, and he promised to return to competition.

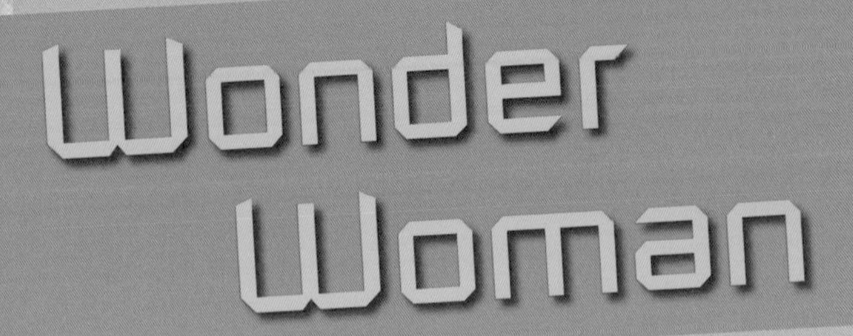

Wonder Woman

Once in a lifetime, an athlete comes along who is much stronger, faster, or just plain better than the rest. He or she leaves the others in the dust. Michael Jordan is like that. But from 1932 until 1954, one name rose above all others. Her name was Mildred Didrikson Zaharias. But she was known to everyone as Babe.

Didrikson married professional wrestler George Zaharias. It was said that she liked how he could drive a golf ball farther than she could!

Didrikson was great at nearly everything she tried. She won a state fair prize for sewing at age 16. And she was a master typist, too!

Nickname

Babe earned her nickname as a child when she hit five home runs in one baseball game. Her friends started to call her Babe after the great baseball slugger of the time, Babe Ruth.

Didrikson was born in 1911 and grew up playing every sport she could. She shone in track and field. She won top medals in eight of nine track events at the National Championships. She made second place in the ninth event! She then won medals in three different Olympic events in 1932. They included hurdles, javelin toss, and high jump. What's more amazing is by 1940, Babe became what many call the greatest woman golfer ever. One day, she decided to take up the sport, and before she knew it, she was the best. She went from track and field champ to the top spot in pro golf. Among her greatest achievements was winning 17 major golf tournaments in a row! She became so good that she was named Woman Athlete of the Half Century.

Secretariat

Amazing physical feats? You don't have to look much further than the powerful racehorse, Secretariat. Besides winning the prestigious Triple Crown, Secretariat won the Belmont Stakes in 1973 by 31 lengths—a seemingly impossible and never replicated feat. No horse has even come close.

One-Shot Disaster

Some athletes handle pressure well. Others choke. In 1989, Scott Hoch needed one final putt to win the Masters Tournament—he missed. Despite being a successful pro golfer for 30 years, he is asked about this missed swing nearly everywhere he goes.

Babe Didrikson

Weird and Wild Feats

Most people may not be able to walk thousands of feet above the ground, jump over cars, or lift hundreds of pounds. But that doesn't mean they can't test the limits of the human body. Check out these amazing tales. Each one is seriously strange but true.

What a Mouthful!

Austrian Marco Hort held 259 drinking straws in his mouth during the World Records Day in 2006.

Epic Lengths!

Xie Qiuping has been growing her hair since 1973. Measuring in at more than 18 feet, her hair is believed to be the longest in the world.

Stuffed!

Around the world, people compete to see how much they can eat. Some people gobble up pies. Others stuff themselves with pizza. In 2009, Takeru Kobayashi (ta-KEH-roo ko-bah-YAH-shee) ate 64.5 hot dogs in 10 minutes.

That Burns!

Have you ever burned your mouth on a hot piece of pizza? Fire eaters use their mouths to quickly put out flames before they can cause any damage.

Only If You Try

How do you reach the top...or fall miserably to the bottom? Only one way! Amazing physical feats and failures all start with a person thinking "I can do it!" and then giving it a good try. **Laurels** come to the victors. And heartache and even broken bones may come to the losers. But losers with a victor's heart try again. To reach the mountaintop, you have to take the first step.

"You may have a fresh start any time you choose, for this thing we call 'failure' is not in the falling down, but in the staying down."

—Mary Pickford, actress

Hits and Misses

Our bodies can accomplish amazing things. It may be painful. It may take years. But for those who don't give up, the feeling of victory is unforgettable.

1932

Babe Didrikson wins medals in three different Olympic events.

1974

Philippe Petit walks between the Twin Towers.

1992

Runner Derek Redmond struggles to reach the finish line with his father.

STOP! THINK...

- Why do you think each of these feats was important?
- What feat do you wish you had accomplished?
- What failures do you think led to these feats?

1996

Kerri Strug overcomes extreme pain to secure the gold medal for her team.

2008

Michael Phelps wins an amazing eight gold medals in swimming.

Tomorrow
What's next?

Glossary

coma—the state of being unconscious and nonresponsive for an extended period of time

daredevil—a person who loves physical thrills and challenges

determination—the desire to accomplish something, no matter what

efficient—capable of producing results without wasted time or energy

feat—a great accomplishment

impulses—urges

laurels—leafy crowns made of the laurel plant and given to athletic champions in ancient Greece; also meaning honors that go to winners

motivational—inspiring

polio—a severe virus that affects the nerves and spinal cord and can result in deformity and loss of muscle use

preliminaries—the competitions leading up to the final competition

prosthetic—artificial or fake

scout—a person sent out to get information, in this case information about top athletes

semifinal—the competition before the final competition

victory—the overcoming of an opponent

Index

Bibliography

Harrington, Geri. ***Jackie Joyner-Kersee: Champion Athlete*. Chelsea House Publications, 1995.**

Learn about one of the world's finest athletes who avoided using prescription drugs to control her asthmatic attacks and overcame many obstacles to become a four-time Olympic champion.

Macceca, Stephanie. ***Wilma Rudolph: Against All Odds.* Teacher Created Materials, 2010.**

This is a biography of the African-American woman who overcame polio as a child to become the first woman to win three gold medals in track and field in a single Olympics.

Milton, Joyce. ***Greg Louganis: Diving for Gold.* Random House Books for Young Readers, 1989.**

This book covers Louganis' shyness, stuttering, and reading problems along with his determination and love of diving.

Zuehlke, Jeffrey. ***Michael Phelps (Amazing Athletes).* 21st Century, 2009.**

This book is about one of the most talked-about American athletes at the 2004 Olympic Games. It follows his days as a talented seven-year-old up to his amazing performance at the 2008 Olympic Games.

More to Explore

Guinness Wold Records

http://www.guinnessworldrecords.com

Meet the latest record breakers and the people who hold some of the craziest titles in the world like hairiest teenager.

Olympic Games

http://www.olympic.org

Read about all the athletes who have medaled in the Olympic Games since 1896, and learn about some of the world's most fascinating sports.

Ted Talks

http://www.ted.com/talks/lang/en/aimee_mullins_prosthetic_aesthetics.html

Check out Aimee Mullins's 12 pairs of legs, and find out how she has used her special legs to inspire others in this video.

ESPN

http://www.espn.go.com/sportscentury/athletes.html

Check out ESPN's list of the top 100 athletes of the century. Did your favorite make the cut?

About the Author

Dona Herweck Rice grew up in Anaheim, California, and graduated from the University of Southern California with a degree in English and from the University of California at Berkeley with a credential for teaching. She has been a teacher in preschool through tenth grade, a researcher, a librarian, and a theater director, and is now an editor, a poet, a writer of teacher materials, and a writer of books for children. She is married with two sons and lives in Southern California. She loves challenging her body to accomplish new feats and is never afraid to try again after a failure.